Rivers of Living Water   by Alan J. Clarredge   I

Prologue!

Standing transfixed, I was amazed by the large number of small planes leaving the main runway of this, the largest private aerodrome in central Zimbabwe. My thoughts regarding my sanity, to say the least, were somewhat confused, wondering, if in the first place, I had been right to put myself in the predicament I now found myself in.

It was February 1987 and whilst attempting to collect my thoughts, the warm fragrant summer air wafted up from the strangely discoloured tar macadam beneath my feet, its stench catching my nostrils with a heady mixture of hot gasoline and flowering hibiscus shrubs. Cooled only a little by a southern breeze, skimming across the runway from the golden low veldt which stretched out for many miles.

The pollen in the air gently irritated my nose, causing the odd sneeze or two. The slight but almost imperceptible temperature difference was just enough to give me goose pimples between the turn-ups of my shorts and the high woollen khaki socks I was wearing (*the traditional leg wear worn in southern Africa since the early 1800s*). My stocking tops were neatly turned over, in the same way I recollect, as a schoolboy growing up during the forties and early fifties.

The goose pimples may have been caused by other reasons, for I was standing with my right thumb raised in the air, waving it to and fro in the time honoured way of thumbing a lift!

Feeling not a little embarrassed I asked myself what idiot would try to get a plane to stop and give him a lift to a land totally embroiled in civil war?

That idiot was me!

I like many, whom I hope and trust will read this little biographical paperback, will have reached that stage in life which the majority of the population, irrespective of nationality, would call their 'Middle Years'. Some might even call it their *'muddle years'*, with no children left at home, second generation school runs for the grandchildren, keep fit reminders on the television and warnings in the newspapers about every type of food we seem to eat and enjoy! It is with no surprise at times and in many different ways a sense of insecurity as to what life could hold in the future.

One major difference I have found at this stage of my life, is the privilege of being able to reflect over many years of life experiences, lots of problems of my own making, but even greater blessings received from God's hand.

Through it all, I have grown in faith and can now say, in the realisation that most things are out of my hands, I am learning *to 'cast all my care upon the Lord'* and leaving all my worries and cares in God's hand. The plan that has presented itself to my memory, and not surprisingly, with strong clarity leaves me with no doubt but to conclude that it has been '*God's Divine Will*' and it is through this that I am certain that I have been divinely directed for my seventy years.

I have learnt through extraordinary happenings, the power of the God of Creation, gentle for some of the time, but overall and too often by far for my comfort, a much stronger influence than I can logically describe. However I am under no doubt that it has only been through His power that I was allowed to perform works that I could never have accomplished in my own strength.

This is not an adventure story in the deep sense of the normal expectancy of a work of fiction, but an adventure, brought about solely through the supernatural Power of the Almighty! I have deeply considered what I have to offer to my readers and I trust that by writing this account of the many God given circumstances in my life, in some small way it may help others. Possibly it may be encouraging for those working and seeking to serve God both at home and overseas, perhaps it will ignite a flame in someone's life that has been extinguished a long time ago.

Please remember that I am attempting to describe my own, very individual introduction to the 'Hand of God', in the sharing of His intervention through many and varied episodes personally experienced.

At nine years of age I firmly believe I was called to serve God in Africa.

The call came during a morning Sunday School class at a tiny Baptist church in the small Dorset town of Wimborne, It was the Baptist Missionary Society weekend and I can still clearly recollect my teacher talking about the Belgian Congo.

Wimborne Baptist Church 2004

Miss Tilley, for that was her name, had provided us with a sticker book containing many blank spaces, these to be filled weekly with picture stamps. The stamps were one old penny each in aid of the Baptist Missionary Society, and after a number of weeks when the brochure was filled, the completed picture showed a colourful native village, full with busy, brightly clothed children playing outside their roundel-thatched houses.

Even at that young age my heart went out to those people.

Rivers of Living Water   by Alan J. Clarredge $

At 24 years of age, I became engaged and married a lovely Christian girl named Lilian from Southampton in Hampshire. In our early years of marriage we moved to the beautiful Priory town of Christchurch in Dorset. It was here that as a happily married man I was blessed with two children, a boy Simon and a girl Amanda.

Then being miraculously motivated by God, during my children's teen years I was taken half way round the world, dodging bombs and ambushes to serve in the war torn city of Beira in Mozambique, continuing to work as a water technologist in medical units throughout Zimbabwe. During my service there I set up wards and fitted equipment for the many people suffering from kidney failure, including the Zimbabwean President's wife Sally Mugabe, a lovely Christian woman until her death.

Over a number of years my work not only involved water purification and kidney unit work in Zimbabwe, but also in Egypt where I toured the military hospitals and advised on kidney dialysis, as well as South Africa advising on water treatment in the township of Soweto, *(towards the end of apartheid)* and Botswana to a water treatment company involved in digging wells in the mighty Kalahari Desert. I witnessed with my own eyes the needs of so many people in this vast continent.

What seemed to be small incidents at the time, certainly led to a much greater story that has touched my life, and I trust, many other lives through the work. I hope and pray this vocation that I have been called into will continue to touch and challenge the lives of others.

Even now as an ordained Minister in a small United Reformed Church in Bournemouth, life has not stopped, and along with the day to day work of the church, the work in Africa has to continue.

Throop United Reformed Church

The birthplace of *Rivers of Living Water*

I am firmly convinced that the work of 'Rivers of Living Water' and its physical and spiritual work has been a response to God's command in Mark 10:42:

"And whosoever shall give to drink unto one of these little ones a cup of cold *water* only in the name of a disciple, verily I say unto you, he shall in no wise lose his reward."

Chapter 1.

The year was 1954 and I received the first spiritual experience that I can remember, in fact one I could never forget. It happened during a film in Wimborne Methodist Church, a Billy Graham film entitled 'Oil town USA'. At what point in the film God spoke to me, I do not know, but in that movie I knew that my life had to be given to God's work and however few my skills, they were to be used for Him.

A faithful mother had made certain I knew about The Lord Jesus Christ from my earliest memory, and now at the age of fourteen I had made a personal commitment. Although not realising it at that precise moment, it turned out to be the commencement of a calling that would allow me so many years of service for the Lord Jesus Christ.

Leaving school two months before my 15th birthday and too young to enter service on the railway, I met a lovely, happy Christian lady called Marjorie Stevens. Unknown to me at that time she had a dreadfully debilitating disease, although, I have to say no mention was ever made of it to myself! It was Marjorie who found me my first temporary job until I was fifteen years old!

This was doing gardening (*not my favourite task, ask Lilian my wife*). It was at a large house in Broadstone in Dorset at which she had been nursing an elderly lady. My only memory apart from Marjorie was buying a bottle of Corona, a quarter of an ounce of liquorice comfits, and a Wagon Wheel daily for my lunch!

In 1955 I had my first experience with water and its wonderful power, working as a fireman on the southern region of British Rail. My childhood delight, as a great number of boys of my generation *(and not a few girls),* had been to be an engine driver. This water, different from what I would be dealing with for the next fifty years, was steam condensed and therefore perfectly clean.

My father *(somewhat wisely)* decided against my own personal preferences, deciding that it would be better for me to become a tradesman than to have no trade and he felt to become a plumber would serve me well for my working life. He did not know it, but the trade I never wanted to be in would give me the opportunity to give life to several Million people for many years ahead. For five years I attended college and learnt many new skills, which, although from a past era, still remain unforgotten and have stood me in good stead.

It was several years later that I found out Marjorie had multiple sclerosis, she never complained, and had a wonderful reputation for going about doing good, she was well loved in her Anglican Church, St Johns at Wimborne.

Whilst still serving my apprenticeship and fitting gutters on a bungalow not a stone's throw from the Steven's house, I met Marjorie's father walking the dog and he told me that his daughter now spent a great deal of time unconscious and how he expected her "to be called Home" that very night.

That evening I went to a prayer meeting at Wimborne Baptist church and we prayed that she would be healed!! Healed? I had never heard of that happening since bible days, but pray they did, and the next day I met Marjorie's dad and almost hesitantly asked how she was. **"She's washing up!"** I was dumbfounded, the last time I saw her, her hands were withered and almost fleshless, bent grossly behind her back, her legs like bean poles had also been hideously twisted!!

I was allowed to meet Marjorie a few days later when the television and newspapers had finished with her. I had the privilege of listening from her own lips to the testimony of just what God had done!

A few weeks before, Marjorie had seen a vision in which she believed that God had said, **"Wait a little while."** These were her own words, **"Whilst I sat strapped in my chair, I felt a glow coming through my body, reaching my hands, the warm circulation helped me to open my fingers, and even gave me enough strength to undo the straps holding me from falling."**

Her eyes, and mine, were wet as she continued to describe this wonderful experience. **"I got out of the chair and walked across the room,"** she demonstrated to me the very actions that had taken place, **"then frightened to scare Mummy and Daddy,"** as she always referred to them, **"I sat down in the chair and called them. They came running, expecting me to be in an unconscious state. By the time they arrived. I had called them and told them not to worry, I got up from the chair and walked to the stairs."**

The staircase in my memory had small, un-equal steps that spiralled to the small lounge and kitchen on the ground floor. **"Halfway down the staircase I wondered why I could not see."** She paused. **"Realising that I was wearing dark glasses to protect my eyes, I spoke to God and said if you have healed me then I don't need these!! And I took them off. My sight was perfect, better than before I was healed."** More tears, more joy, as she said, **"I then washed up for Mummy and Daddy."**

A healing that lasted for fifty years until she was called home a short while ago.   Suddenly and without room left for doubt, I personally realised that God is alive today. Life for me, took on a new meaning.

As if to confirm His mighty power, I too experienced an incident whilst riding my small BSA Bantam motorbike to work one morning.
It was a steep windy road with tall hedgerows prohibiting any form of view of the road ahead. Suddenly, prior to a sharp bend in the road, the machine cut out and I came to a fairly abrupt halt. Immediately a tractor came from a hidden gateway without stopping for the ongoing traffic. God had spared my life!!
The bike re-started instantly and I felt it had to be a miracle, I never found anything wrong with the machine!

Sadly it still took me a few years until I experienced the power of the Holy Spirit in my life and only when I went to a small church in Ringwood in Hampshire called the 'Glory Revival Centre'. Donald Harper was the Pastor there and he introduced me to the Holy Ghost in a very personal way. It was in a Sunday night service that I experienced, as the early disciples, the Baptism in the Holy Ghost, a life changing experience that gave me a spiritual 'fire' and changed my whole way of life.

I was still an apprentice and apart from college studies I regularly attended my Wimborne church in the mornings and Ringwood in the evenings, trusting that one day I would serve God overseas. I even applied to a large missionary society that specialised in serving in the Congo *(as it was called then),* but I was turned down by a sharp and very formal letter on the grounds that my education was not of the level required in their work. I remember the disappointment I felt and could not help but draw the conclusion that small town schools had their drawbacks.

After my apprenticeship I worked for the water board as an inspector in North Dorset for a short time and lodged with a strict Brethren family.

Rivers of Living Water   by Alan J. Clarredge

When I became engaged to Lilian I moved back with my family in Wimborne and worked in Corfe Mullen for a small builder, so I was not too far away from my fiancé in Southampton, whom I visited most evenings. After our marriage at Ringwood, we moved to Bournemouth and attended Lansdowne Baptist Church where I had been baptised in water in 1956 and it was then that I felt the hand of God directing me to the work which He wanted me to do. Work to prepare me for His future.

I was not well paid and also had to travel at least twenty miles a day to work, with petrol at four shillings and sixpence a gallon *(twenty two and a half pence today)* it made quite a dent in my £6.50 per week wages. We decided to pray and at 11pm on the Saturday night before Christmas in 1964 I felt the urge to write to Bournemouth Corporation for a job in their school heating section!
Why, apart from divine guidance, I could not tell you, I had never been involved in heating let alone the scale of knowledge that the schools demanded! I wrote at that moment of time. Within two weeks I had been accepted and started work gaining knowledge in new fields and being near my young family as they were growing up.

God moves in many ways and after a number of years the corporation started to change, as foreman I was involved politically with the alterations and at that time did not recognise God was moving me onto another field. The new boss came and within a few hours explained that he never liked existing staff to remain, and asked when would I leave? I was sad, for in many ways I thoroughly enjoyed my work.

My natural reaction would be to dig my heels in whatever the situation. However, I decided to look for a new job and then I saw an advertisement in a daily newspaper for a service engineer. Its wording interested me, so I applied for a position on a water treatment company. Its name, *'Permutit'*, a household name at that time. My main work would be on water softeners, which the company manufactured in South Wales and later to progress onto a more advanced field of water treatment equipment for specialised work, not realising at that time it would culminate in entering the medical field.

I obtained this position and it was the start of a process that took me into a vocation that taught me skills that I could never have achieved as a plumber and knowledge that would be invaluable when used for the Lord's work.

Many reasons, *(not least finance, or lack of it)* we moved to Christchurch and joined Christchurch Baptist Church, where Lilian played in the worship group and jointly we ran the Young People's Fellowship. God moved in a wonderful way and young people came in from every direction, they were saved *(found Jesus Christ as their Lord and Saviour)* filled with the Holy Spirit, were baptised in water and in turn grew in their faith.

One testimony to both the Church and the young people came in 1977, when I was giving a talk at Yeovil General Hospital about water treatment and demonstrating how sulphuric acid was used in cleaning their filtration equipment. Whilst I was talking, a faint layer of acrid gas filled the air around the small group I was lost in my delivery when suddenly I realised it was acid, a carboy above my head had sprung a fine leak and the liquid in the container was discharging in a fine spray over the lower half of my body. Within a few seconds my brown corduroy trousers started to 'melt'.

The acidic fumes singed the hairs from my nostrils and instantly I realised what had happened. Without wasting time I looked for the required water hose to douse myself, none! Not even a tap. The men panicked more than I, they quickly rushed me into the toilet, dipping each foot in the pan then pulling the chain, this meant little consolation, for we all realised that the sweet cooling of the water covered such a tiny area of the fast spreading contamination of my body.

My fear started when I was put in a wheelchair and rushed down the steepest alleyway beside the boiler house that I had ever seen and towards the emergency ward. I watched as the main road between the boiler house and the hospital loomed before me. It was fear of the road, not the acid.
Once we had crossed the road and they had not lost control of the wheelchair I was at peace, no waiting in casualty here, straight onto a bed in the emergency ward.

The doctor had a long bladed scissor and made to cut the black shrivelled skin from my leg, she apologised by saying I was very badly burnt. I felt no fear at this point and against all logic told the doctor that I was all right! I am certain she thought I was mad, but she did not say so. After this she started to pull at the black substance on my legs, and miraculously not even one hair was destroyed!! I did not have time to pray, but the Sunday following this incident I held up the remains of my trousers (*which looked typical of the imaginary ones in Robinson Crusoe*) before the whole church as a testimony of what God had done!!

The work amongst the young people flourished and then came the next step in moving me on to further work for God.

Shock, for in October 1977 during the evening service I had the most terrible indigestion, *(or so I thought)* it was a coronary and by the end of the evening the young people had called a prayer meeting whilst Lilian and my son waited outside the coronary care unit at Boscombe hospital in Bournemouth.

The time had come for me to change direction yet once again!

Permutit had been good to me throughout my illness and after recovering I was soon doing the normal work plus running the office in Shepton Mallet for long periods. It was at this time that the next major episode in my life took place, not pleasant at the time, but faith building to the extreme.

I developed a medical condition called peripheral neurophomy, and totally hated the pain of the increasing electrical impulses injected through me whilst attending the neurology department of Southampton General Hospital *(where my wife had once been a nurse).* This is given to read the speed of the sensory nerves from the brain to the extremities *(such as was in my case, the tips of the fingers).*

So for the next year at three monthly intervals, I received fresh tests, my tools which I could not hold firmly slipped frequently from my hands, my co-ordination became confused, and my shoes dragged on the ground when I walked, wearing them out within a matter of weeks.
I thought of Marjorie Stevens and remembered how God had healed her. The church prayed and one Job's comforter talked to Lilian and said a chairlift would soon be required for our house.

It most certainly was not God's will

Within a few months I received a telephone call from my head office asking if I would apply for a job that was being sent to all engineers, the position advertised was for that of technical advisor to the domestic division of the company *(They had no idea of any health problems other than my coronary).*

I sought advice from a number of the elders in our church and they felt that under the circumstances it would be most unwise to apply for the position. I still felt uncertain as to their advice and decided to pursue the matter a little further, giving God the chance to close the door if He wanted to. I realised that if I took the position I would not have to use my hands in the way I had done for many years and the ever increasing symptoms would not cause me undue stress. I also knew that God could heal my body, what a quandary.

Lilian and I both prayed and we agreed that I should apply for the position and if it was God's will I would be offered the position!
I was offered the post and given just ten minutes to make up my mind, this was enough time to contact Lilian and then to give them my reply!   We both said yes.

The implication of the change of occupation did not dawn upon me immediately, two weeks from that date I had to move to London and find somewhere to live. I contacted local churches and visited agencies over the next two weeks and drew a blank every time. I began to question my interpretation of the way ahead, had the elders been correct?

On the Friday prior to starting my new position in London I visited some very elderly friends and to my surprise they had a visitor staying with them. She too was elderly, and did not speak. Her eyes were heavy from crying and I managed to ask one of the sisters with whom she was staying, what the problem was.

Wynn, for that was her name, was a lovely Christian lady who regularly attended West Ealing Baptist Church. I discovered she had just lost her husband Les and the poor soul just could not face going back to an empty house. That empty house was in Altenburgh Avenue, Ealing not more than one mile from my new post!! She didn't need to go back to an empty house on that Monday morning, God had given her a companion and me a roof over my head!! For a small rent my accommodation was assured for the foreseeable future.   Not only that but she treated me as the son she never had.

Sadly I nursed her in the last weeks of her life, as within six months of my moving in she passed away with cancer. God had placed me there for her comfort as well as my security.

Within a few hours of the funeral I had a telephone call from her family whom I had not met, and I believe did not see her very often. **"How soon can you leave the house? We are going to sell it"**! I was shocked! By this time I was engrossed in a new learning cycle and the disruption, let alone the cost, would be almost impossible.

I prayed! Within twenty four hours it was discovered that no will existed, and although Wynn intended after I had no more use for the accommodation to leave the house to a missionary society, her wishes were un-written and therefore not observed by her family.

However, they were forced by circumstances to ask me to stay and look after the house until probate was concluded, *rent free*!! God provides and it took well over a year for all the legalities to be met.

I only needed temporary accommodation after that as I was now travelling for the company from our home in Dorset. A friend of Wynn lent me her house, so whenever I needed to stay in London I had a place to stay!! Added to the blessing of the secured accommodation, the disease of the nerves had stopped progressing and totally disappeared. I must add that for the last thirty years it has never returned, nor do I think it ever will!!

My work as technical advisor changed and it was decided that the company was to enter the medical field of kidney dialysis.

My job would involve adapting equipment for this very important task. I was sent to Liverpool University Hospital where I studied the technology of kidney dialysis and a few poor patients had to survive my handling of their blood supply! I will not waste time on what happened during that period, except, I eventually became medical advisor to the company. Having always been interested in the medical world I slipped into the role with ease and not a little trepidation.

Rumours had spread throughout the company that the future may not be as secure as I imagined and when I stopped at the services near Leeds high on the M1, it was a complete surprise when the man who had to share my coffee table through lack of space in the busy café, turned out to be employed by a rival company, who were also in the kidney dialysis field.

They were looking for a new technician!! I left my address with him. Culligan, for that was the name of the company *(part of a water treatment firm from the USA),* wrote to me within three days asking if I would come and see them. I took the plunge and went for an interview at High Wycombe. I was offered the position of medical advisor to the company and accepted *(my department at Permutit was closed down within six months of me leaving the firm).* In the meantime I had moved back to Christchurch.

For the past few years not only was I working away from home in Christchurch, but at weekends Lilian and myself were pastoring the little church in Ringwood, Hampshire where we were married.

Don Harper was retiring and he had passed his mantle on to us. Life was not dull and for a few years we were greatly blessed at Ringwood, complete with a chapter of 'hell's angels' from Wolverhampton who called in possibly to cause havoc one Sunday afternoon but found more than they had ever bargained for, ending up finding the Saviour of their lives, Jesus! They moved as one to Ringwood and became the backbone of the Church.

Then the fellowship received a shock, the executors of the hall decided to get rid of the building and close us down. God's timing is perfect.

He knew exactly what was happening and we spent four weeks

introducing our young church members into other Christian groups whilst having a meeting in our house so as to give continuity to their faith. Every person and family settled down during this period in a Church near their homes.

Perfect timing for at the end of my first month with Culligan, I was asked to go to Harare for an exhibition. Harare? I had never heard of the place, it was not in my atlas. If they had said Salisbury, Southern Rhodesia, then I would have known. The name of Harare was very new, following recent independence from Britain. I was not as yet familiar with the political changes sweeping throughout that part of southern Africa.

During the next twenty years or so, I was to witness changes in history that were unbelievable and totally unforeseeable at that time.

I felt elated as I took my first flight on a Boeing 707 Air Zimbabwe plane and alighted at Harare International airport on a beautiful summer morning. Although there for only eight days, I was at last going to the continent in which I still believed God had work for me.

Culligan had been extremely vague about my accommodation and just told me it was called 'The Harare Club'. I soon discovered this vagueness was not unusual, especially in this part of southern Africa, and for the first few years I worked in the country I had to learn to become totally reliant on finding places and people that the local agents had arranged for me to visit.
It did lead to problems, as the taxi man had only heard of Harare Cricket Club and this at 6.30am in the morning was where we ended up. After a lot of enquiries by my taxi driver we arrived at the correct Harare Club.

It was a 'gentleman's club' in the traditional Colonial sense and a suit had to be worn at all times. The accommodation struck me very much as I would have imagined a university room to have been like, with the small bedroom containing a wash hand basin, single wardrobe and bed, on a small desk stood a small brass bell, highly polished. I wondered why the bell? The reason I soon discovered being the smartly dressed flunkey that stood at the end of the corridor, awaiting my summons should I, or any other residents need anything!

It was situated in Union Square, a beautiful small park full of purple flowering Jacaranda trees situated in the centre of Harare. The famous Meikles Hotel on one side, whilst 'The Herald' offices, the national newspaper, was on another. On the far side of the square was the Parliament building, the beautiful red brick white colonial design greatly impressed me and caused my first rude encounter with the new regime. Hardly had the shutter closed on my camera when it was relieved of me by an armed guard, I had taken a forbidden picture, not the parliament house, but outside stood an *'elderly ambulance'* and it was intended for the then Prime Minister, Robert Mugabe, should he be taken ill. Grudgingly I handed over the film to be destroyed!

The trip was comical in many ways, for although I held a huge space at the Harare Show, no advertising literature nor products arrived to be put on the stand. Frantically I searched for pictures and posters to put on display and eventually I ended up with a vast picture show of scenes from Victoria falls.
Well it was water! The posters were borrowed from the few travel agents in the city! That, with just a table and two chairs, was the sole effort that I could make for 'Culligan's first African exhibition.

Mr Mugabe & President Gandhi were due to visit me at 2.00pm for an arranged talk by our agents *(One of whom was Senator Sabena Mugabe, the Prime Minister's sister)* regarding water purification in their respective countries.

At twelve 0'clock I left for lunch leaving Passmore, the young African, to mind the stand. 1pm I returned. When 2pm had arrived and gone Passmore unwittingly broke the news to me when I bemoaned the non arrival of the dignitaries he said **"Mr Mugabe and President Gandhi liked the stand"**

I had missed them as they were early, two hours before the arranged time, (*something I never encountered again in Africa, early!!*) and did not see them again. Thankfully on my return to the UK no awkward questions were raised regarding this occurrence and I omitted to inform the company!!

For a few days I visited the Low veldt and saw the vast need for water purification, this challenged me to talk with the company and return as soon as was possible to help the many people in the supply of pure water. It was time to leave and with a huge entourage gathered on the gallery of the airport to wave goodbye I returned to England, tears in my eyes at leaving my new found friends. My heart was well and truly won over for my future work in Africa.

2007 O.Tambo Airport Johannesburg

Chapter 2.

Within three weeks I returned to Zimbabwe, this time for a month to visit several areas of this vast country and meet a number of water board employees. I learnt of the shortages, learnt of the problems and began to be Africanised by the local population.

One incident that sticks out in my mind was a trip to Kariba Dam. The African company I had been sent to work with decided I should meet the officials at this large dam to see if we could become involved in a large project of water purification. The details were very precise and must have cost a fortune to prepare, there were so many noughts on the figures in the quotation that I could never really grasp its true value.

After dropping my colleague's children at school we set off for Kariba, some 200 miles to the west of Harare. We were just fifty miles from our destination when we encountered our first problem! I had to fill up the car with petrol, it was then and only then that Reginald Ghona told me that he had spent the money given to us by his boss!! **"I had to pay school fees for my children!"** I soon learnt this was a typical thing to happen in Zimbabwe. **"You must have money Boss?"** I had enough cash to get us to Kariba and perhaps forty or fifty miles for the return journey, but no more!! We went on to Kariba and Ghona said he had relatives who would give him the money that he had used! Needless to say those relatives had not enough money to keep themselves, let alone their thieving nephew!

My next little problem at Kariba happened so suddenly that I feel the members of the town council who witnessed the incident should have forgiven me more than they did. I go too fast. The town clerk presented me with the plans for the water purification works for my examination and comments *(I have to admit to it being a much larger project than I had ever worked on before and left me perspiring as I looked at the drawings, it of course could have been the 40c temperature that made me sweat!).*

It was very hot and as we were sat in the town hall garden, I carefully scrutinised the only set of plans they possessed on a rickety old table under the shade of several small trees. Without warning, a rather large and extremely aggressive looking baboon ran past me, grabbed the plans from my hand and made off with them with the speed of an express train!!

That was the last we ever saw of those plans to the town clerk's dismay and to my acute embarrassment. As we left the town I half expected to see a large number of monkeys with paper hats on their heads, made out of the plans! We didn't. Forty miles away the petrol gauge reached the red line and we were still some 150 miles from Harare!

My colleague used his ingenuity and at every bus stop we picked up passengers and collected their fares. When we eventually arrived home Ghona turned to me and said, "I made a profit today!!" Like Queen Victoria of old, I was not amused. He was duly sacked by his boss on my recommendation and proceeded to get his own back on me at a later date. How? You may well ask. Well all will be revealed later in my story.

Back to England for a short time and almost immediately I was sent abroad again, to run a church in the UK would have been impossible.

This time to Budapest for a renal conference and it was at this conference that my future changed. I met a man from Zimbabwe, his name was Obadiah Moyo and he told me that he needed me to be in Zimbabwe to oversee a venture that was to be financed by a top official of that country. Once again, I ended up back in that beautiful African country.

After three months of preparation work I gave a quotation for the equipment required to set up five kidney units in different parts of the country and awaited confirmation as to whether they wished me to supply the materials.

Without warning I had an urgent summons back to the UK, it sounded quite serious and I wondered what hot water I had got myself into? On my arrival at 6.30am, I drove straight to the Culligan headquarters in High Wycombe and there I was told that my department was closed and I was surplus to requirements. I was shaken, £200 severance payment, no more Zimbabwe and nothing achieved. Was this the end? I asked myself.

No, certainly not, for within seven days I received a cheque made out to me for the purchase equipment to supply pure water for five new kidney units for the health authority in Zimbabwe.

The Zimbabwe Government arranged my air travel and I was back within a short period of time to await my ordered and paid for equipment to arrive. No work and no wages until work commenced, but feeling secure that the finance for the equipment was paid and sometime I would receive a wage (Zimbabwe dollars) whilst living in a country that was becoming so dear to my heart.

One humorous event was the renting of an apartment for myself and my family during the school holidays. The name stuck out on the advertisement Alan. J. Clarridge (Real Estate) Only one letter difference from my own name - I telephoned. The conversation went like this, **"Clarridge's real estate."** My reply, **"Yes I would like a flat please."** "Name please." "Alan Clarredge." "Yes it's Alan Clarridge." "No I'm Alan Clarredge."** The gentleman who was my namesake let out a sharp breath that I could distinctly hear, **"No I'm Alan Clarridge!"** After a few minutes of persuading the phone was handed over to someone else in the office and a voice said **"Hello**

son." It was Alan's father. Following a long discussion which proved we were not related, I found that no apartments were available.

Out of work in a country which at that time was foreign to me, perhaps I should have been scared of the future! I wasn't, I knew the reason why I fitted in, it was because God had placed me there.

Within a short time I had been given a job within Harare, at one of the oldest buildings in the city. Mitchell's Real Estate, 'Puzey House', Manica Rd *(the name at that time, now Robert Mugabe Way)* Harare, this also provided me with a nice apartment in Harare.

Puzey House, Robert Mugabe Way, Harare

My residency had to be applied for before I could undertake any work and this was obtained from the highest authority because of my specialist work regarding dialysis.

I could now draw a wage legally and this covered the rent of my apartment and the hire of a 'house girl' to do the little chores that I was not able to do: ironing, washing, to name but a few. *(I did cook for myself, mainly steak, for that was the cheapest meat and I was living on Zimbabwe wages.)* The flat was wonderful and enabled Lilian and the children to join me during the school holidays. My house girl used to sit on the front door step waiting for me to leave for work although my wife did not appreciate having to get out of bed for the cleaner to come in at 6.30am and never got used to the idea of being a 'lady of leisure'.

After fellowshipping in a number of good churches I found a church in Hatfield on the outskirts of Harare. It was a small Assemblies of God, and the pastor's name was Philip Chigomi. We became great friends over the years and it was not long before I joined him in the work, even though at most times it meant a walk of five miles to the church, starting at 7am to enable me to reach the church for the 10am. service each Sunday morning. It was inspiring and also an opportunity to meet local people. Eventually I received my credentials from the denomination to become a pastor and became joint overseer with him at his request! It also helped me considerably for I received a small stipend.

The next test of faith came when the equipment, ordered by myself and paid for by the Government failed to arrive. I enquired daily at the courier's office when it would arrive. Each time I was told that it would be here tomorrow, tomorrow never came. I felt a cold chill run down my spine, when I was eventually told that there had been a fire in England and every item I had bought had been destroyed in the fire!!

My daughter and my accountant in England chased the company to see if they had insured it and they said it was my responsibility. The cost, over £38,000, this at the time would have meant selling our house in the UK. What could I do? The church in Throop who supported me with prayer, prayed! Lilian who was with me at the time as only to be expected was just as concerned as I.

Naturally the Zimbabwe Government was pressurising me over the receiving of the equipment and I was having visions of ending up in Chikarubi, (the worst prison I had been told) in Zimbabwe. I did the only thing I could, I re-ordered the equipment and arranged for it to arrive by air. Thankfully the company did not ask for payment up front.

Lilian can vouch for the next miraculous thing that took place. For twelve weeks I had this huge concern hanging over me like a black cloud, until one morning, *(I can indelibly remember it),* the time 3am and lying fully awake I felt strangely compelled to go to my office, (*a small wardrobe in the spare bedroom, with papers laying flat on each other standing for at least five foot in height*).

For some reason I fished out a small pile of quotes and papers from the centre of the heap and there, although I had looked on numerous occasions, was the original quote and on the paper were the words that saved the situation, "F.O.B." Free On Board, which indicated I was not responsible for re-supplying the equipment!!

Peace at last and I felt a further faith building test had been overcome. All this time my trust was growing, not only through this occasion, but also on numerous minor occurrences such as the revenge of Ghona! It happened when I was returning for a short break in the UK, all went well, Lilian and myself had reached the airport and passed through customs control. The customs officials sit at a high wooden desk in the centre of the corridor, screens divided the way ahead, as alternately the passengers split and went through the barrier, first traveller to the left, second to the right and so on. Lillian took the right passageway to the terminal building and I the left. Lilian entered the terminal alone!

As I passed the stern faced customs officer, a hidden door behind me silently opened, a hand grasped by shoulder and I was drawn into a long, well lit room. The door closed behind me. The white official sat at a small desk looking at an extremely large folder, I clearly saw my name on the top. I asked myself how in just a few years could I accumulate such a large dossier? Immediately he started to throw questions at me, some relevant, most not. None were racial but something about the tone of the questioning made me deeply suspicious!

It could only have been some form of discernment when my ex employee came to my mind and the moment I heard the phrase *"living off immoral earnings"* I knew it could only have been the vindictive and lying tongue of Reginald Ghona.

I explained the reason behind his dismissal and a phone call was made to an extremely high official. Within two minutes, I was in the terminal building alongside my wife who had not even realised there had been a problem.

One opportunity came my way when the pastor of another local church, whom I was involved with, was invited to give the morning thought on the national radio station, *ZBC (Zimbabwe Broadcasting Corporation)* for Independence day 1987. He phoned me the night before and said he would like me to do the morning service and asked me to step in for him. I felt very inadequate for this situation, yet God gave me the words as He always does and I had the opportunity as a white man to congratulate them and give the gospel in this new and at that time vibrant country.

I remember addressing the Prime Minister (*Robert Mugabe prior to becoming President)* on air that we can be independent of England, but not of God. I was not arrested or criticised in this so called communist country, but instead given many opportunities to broadcast and talk of water, linking it with a spiritual application on numerous occasions. In fact I even stood in for a disc jockey and took the Zimbabwe version of 'top of the pops', thank goodness their songs were still in the era of the British forties and fifties.

To give the gospel is not illegal in this so called communist country, in fact it could be said to be encouraged, uncontaminated with a lot of the evils from the west. Through this, a strong Christian influence prevailed on both radio and television in Zimbabwe *(proving invaluable to my work in Mozambique)*.

The work in the various hospitals progressed and gradually I saw more and more equipment and materials arriving in the shops. Instead of queuing at the builders' merchants for several hours each day I knew where to go, no more 'chewing gum' to seal pipes as we had been forced to use a couple of years previous (*a very different picture than 2010 when it has returned to 'chewing gum'*).

The units were in use and I needed a break.

Abel Waldman with Reverse osmosis equipment purifying water Mpilo hospital HIV dept. Bulawayo

Not the case, for a local evangelist phoned me and asked if I could come with him to Beira in Mozambique were they desperately needed water in a missionary house. I took my life in my hands and went along the Beira corridor, at that time reputed to be the most dangerous road in Africa! I had never seen 'mined pot holes', the size that existed on that dusty uneven road.

Beira Corridor Mozambique

My job was to watch for the tell-tell signs of these traps by looking for a darker surface than the normal road, for over eighty kilometres I strained my eyes in an endeavour for us not to be grounded or blown up by the strangely camouflaged traps.

At one point we passed a ten tonne lorry whose bonnet was buried in the ground some three to four feet deep, there could be no lapse in our vigilance.

Potholes on the way to Beira

Rivers of Living Water by Alan J. Clarredge

Arrival in Beira was an eye opener, wide dirt streets, ending as suddenly as we entered them, no road signs of any description. The road to the sea front where the missionary house 'lay' was precarious to say the least. Instead of pot holes, we were now looking to see if any more immediate dangers prevailed, such as 'bandits', the Felimo opposition to the ruling communist government.

Politics seem to be the main adversary of so many African states, yet if we are honest nothing has changed through history. We have heard of wars and rumours of war since time began it's no wonder they needed a Saviour and we still do!

Missionary house Beira seafront

We arrived at the house and my description of the property could only be that it 'laid' on the beautiful white sanded beach, with the Indian Ocean lapping its edge. The house, although magnificent in some past era, was bereft of a back, as this had been reclaimed by the breakers and lay upon the sand, with the beautiful clear water lapping over the limpet strewn bricks.
My job was to put water in this building so as any missionaries working at the hospital might have accommodation. Lilian and myself

did not feel that to put water in a house built upon sand was a very good investment, as did the Welsh bricklayer who shared our conviction and continuously muttered as he laid his bricks, **"Unscriptural, unscriptural, building on sand!"**

Whilst carrying out a survey of the house I was taken down the road to Beira hospital and from that visit the organisation 'Rivers of Living Water' was unintentionally started. Not a name thought of by myself, but the name suggested back in the UK by Roger our house group leader at Throop United Reformed Church in 1987.

Beira Hospital front facade

Beira Hospital catered for up to 2000 patients at any one time, it was large, bereft of equipment, bare in decoration and acutely short of beds. The maternity ward was my first port of call, two patients per bed, top story, two patients under the bed!! My heart turned to jelly as I watched a long haired rat race over the body of a fly covered patient on the floor, followed by the animal's kith and kin when at least three smaller animals followed in the creature's footsteps!

I would not mind spiders normally, but this huge arachnid supporting itself in the web that stretched over the maternity ward door had a span of over six inches in width I could see the majority of its eight eyes and it possessed a beak the size of a small bird, *(which I am certain it relied upon)*. Each time we entered or left the building we had to duck beneath this hairy creature, It was left undisturbed, or so I was told, to eat the many varieties of insect and small bird life that interfered with the running of the hospital.

Outside the hospital were long queues that held in excess of 200 people, these I was told were waiting for one drip of water per minute from a rusty tap in the hospital grounds. The water was salty and I guess straight from the Indian Ocean. The rusty tin cans into which the discoloured liquid dripped did nothing for the health, and I would have thought, patience of the people queuing for many hours in the hot, humid air. With this quality of water it was no wonder the babies that were delivered had to be cleaned with 'Savlon' donated from many countries.

My heart went out to these people, some years ago when the Portuguese left the country they broke most of the equipment in the land and with the bitter civil war, the rest was now destroyed!

Matilda was the matron of Beira hospital and she had nothing but headaches with the day to day running of the establishment. Very little food, no water, no toilet facilities, very little medicine and what was there was out of date *(donated by a large UK chemist)*. She and her husband, a customs official, had asked me back to their once spacious house, now with no electricity and fuel, the floor boards had been raised, and in the middle of the kitchen floor a small fire burned, the pot on top of the fire contained a form of stew.
I was hungry, in fact we were all hungry and that python stew tasted better than anything I had eaten for the past week. They even offered

me a second helping!

Matilda presented me with a small ornament, hand carved from ebony, explaining that national treasures were not allowed out of the country (*when I returned to Zimbabwe, her husband wrote me a customs note to take it out*!)

Now I felt I could do nothing less than to tell the smiling matron of the hospital, in whose house I was eating probably the last of the food, that I would get water on for that hospital!

Words are all too easy, action is something different!

The Mozambique government put me up at the hotel Ambassador whilst I prepared my plans to restore water to the hospital. It was a multi floored building and I was on the eleventh floor, no windows remained in the hotel, without exception all had been blown out at some time, no electricity so no lifts and when I entered the dining room I could not believe my eyes, for all the guests carried minute lunch boxes and proceeded to eat. I had no food. I have to say that I was thankful for the half a cup of warm water that was provided, although it may have been very weak tea, the stale taste prohibited me from recognising anything that I was drinking.

At about six 0'clock in the evening I went to bed, as it was pitch dark and there were no lights, there was nothing else I could do, my clothes were draped wherever I could find a space on the floor *(there were no cupboards or even a chair)*. I felt sure that by placing them on the floor they would have been full of creepy creatures yet there was nothing I could do about it. The blankets had holes in them, as did the sheets. The stifling humidity restricted my breathing and I was glad to shut my eyes. Sometime during the evening I was awoken by a loud banging on the door, it was a pastor from the local Baptist church, **"come on, come on"** he was saying. Gathering my wits and my clothes was a struggle, as together we walked down the many flights of stairs, I suffer from night blindness and this good brother did not let go of me for one moment! With no banisters I could have plunged down the stairwell beside those stairs for sixty feet at least.

Once outside in the hot humid air we walked briskly to the railway arches, through a doorway into a large tunnel that stretched a good seventy to a hundred yards beneath the station and the tracks. Inside I could see by the gleam of countless candles, trestle tables stretching as far as the eye could see. The tables contained huge black saucepans and before long hundreds and hundreds of people began to enter the shelter. King prawns by the hundred were removed from the innumerable pots and every person in the city that came received enough food to fill them to overflowing! Afterwards we sang hymns of praise to a bountiful God. Once they were starving now they were full!

I worked for the rest of the week and on the Sunday I was invited to speak at the Baptist church. About three hundred people met for worship, there was not a space in the church and even the window ledges were filled with smiling children I spoke with the aid of an interpreter and afterwards it was decided to have a 'glory march' through the city and down to the sea front. The people walked hand in hand singing choruses which although in Portuguese were easily recognised by the tune, the blind falling into drains with cracked lids and being pulled out, we even stopped to climb six floors in an unlit flat to pray for a little baby suffering from malnutrition and possible Pneumonia.

We eventually stopped outside the Russian Embassy, a huge gun sat opposite the building on the sea shore, strangely pointing at the embassy!! By this time there must have been a good thousand or so people gathered, these people, including myself joined hands and encircled the whole building two deep. They prayed and sang, louder and louder. I was surprised the guards did not come out of the embassy and shoot us, thankfully they didn't.

The Russians had come into the land to protect the communist government, but instead of that they robbed the country of any wealth that it had, including their food. The prayers it turned out were for the oppressors to leave! Next morning several dozen army lorries turned up at the embassy, they loaded their goods and off they went, not to return!!

Yet once again I found God does answer prayer! I returned to Zimbabwe and then back to the UK.

In the UK I wrote to dozens of churches around Bournemouth, Christchurch and Poole areas, and other organisations asking for a voluntary gift of £10-£20 and the money came in.

In my search for the right equipment I visited many water projects and purification works in many areas of Britain, eventually purchasing enough equipment to give a good water supply to Beira hospital.

Side façade of Beira Hospital

Now how was I to send the equipment overseas? Somebody suggested Tear Fund and sure enough if I could get my equipment to Sevenoaks in Kent, then they would ship it to Beira port for me.

The BBC filmed us loading up the equipment in Christchurch and off it went.

Chapter 3.

On my return to Zimbabwe I was kept very busy in the church and working on small hospital projects for several months.

One memorable and very humorous occasion happened during the period approaching Christmas 1994, it was a special Saturday service in October to celebrate Christmas. The young people did a presentation against the evils of *drink (we call it binge drinking today).* Pastor Chigomi's son was the principle actor, he was standing behind a portable pulpit, with the other young people sitting on a row of chairs in front of the dais. He raised his hands imitating his father whilst preaching and then told the congregation to bow their heads in prayer. Whilst bowed, he reached beneath the pulpit and picked up a bottle of 'Castle Lager' *(empty I am certain).* He took a swig at the bottle and then hid it again before the prayer was over, this was done several times in quick succession, indicating I think the evil of secret drinking! The whole dialogue was in Shona the native language of the area and I did not understand a word, yet the message could not have been plainer.

My part was next, to slip behind the curtain and play the carols for the evening, my programme showed each carol and I played loudly, singing to myself those lovely words. My embarrassment only came when I had finished and they still had one song left!!   ***I do not think anyone noticed!!***

I took the opportunity each Christmas to cook a meal for the church members, this year it was goat. "Very tasty, very nice!" to quote a certain NCO in the BBC series called Dad's Army.

There was one problem, I cooked lots and lots of meat well minced and very hot and smelly, it was all prepared for the 5 mile journey from my flat to the church at Hatfield. My car was far more 'holy' than righteous, the yellow Ford Anglia which had become very familiar to the folks of Harare was full of rusty holes, allowing water to enter the vehicle and cool us down in the rainy season, although Lilian did not appreciate it in her Sunday best!

On the roof a 'Castrol' oil gallon can roosted, with an attached tube feeding the dip stick to top up the oil as the blue and somewhat smelly haze filled the air behind the automobile. The car with 190,000 kms on the clock was somewhat temperamental and it was into this little vehicle I tightly packed the dishes of goat's meat. The aroma, if you could call it that, was rather strong! In those days police checks were set up randomly at two mile intervals and just a few hundred yards from my flat in Avondale, North Harare I was stopped. Not only me, but also the engine stopped, as my papers were examined, a queue built up behind me when the 'yellow peril' refused to start.

The nickname given to me by Gladys, one of the local residents, had been 'disaster' because of Mozambique and the number of times I was being called to failures in the water supplies of the country. This was a minor disaster in proportion to those, but the humidity and stench in the car had risen to a level that even I could not bear. I stood beside the car and addressed the smartly uniformed police officer, **"It's your fault"** I accused the poor fellow, **"What are you going to do? The poor people in my church at Hatfield are waiting for this food and now you have made me break down."**

There was an earnest conversation between the officers, I was firmly blocking the road and a large number of drivers were clearly beginning to get extremely annoyed.

Then something took place that would never have happened in the

Rivers of Living Water   by Alan J. Clarredge   **38**

UK.

A chain was removed from the back of the ancient *(not quite so ancient as my car)* police vehicle, the officer attached the chain to my car and then to the back of the police vehicle, immediately he left the other two officers at the road block and towed me the five miles to the church at Hatfield!! The most humorous thing then happened, the officer did not leave straight away, but stayed for the meal, only returning to his colleagues after he had eaten sufficient!!

The next memorable thing was during a broadcast with Colin Harvey, a well known national television and radio producer and presenter. It was during a live broadcast that I felt the urge to ask members of the audience if anyone could get me to Beira to visit the hospital to help with the water problem. A somewhat stupid request considering a full scale civil war was taking place in Mozambique, yet it seemed that I was divinely led, for apart from a few listeners asking me to bring back king prawns, one lady said that if I booked up a plane from missionary aviation she would pay for it.

I could have danced around the studio, in fact I was so excited I failed to ask the producer to take her phone number or name. The next day I hired the plane, £500, and I assured them it would be paid for by my anonymous donor. One problem, that anonymous donor remained anonymous and never contacted me again.

I phoned missionary aviation and told them, they duly cancelled the plane. I asked them "**what can I do?**" the helpful young Canadian suggested that I **"hitchhike"**. I retorted **"No cars go to Beira, only army lorries, they won't give me a lift!"** "**No, at the airport,**" he stated. Hence the prologue to this story.

I felt strongly compelled to do as he said, totally against my personality.

I obtained a visa, packed my suitcase and set of for **Charles Prince International Airport** on the northern perimeter of the city. At 8am I was standing beside the runway thumbing a lift.

To this day it seems unbelievable that I should ever attempt to do this and yet I did!! I stood for less than ten minutes when a very tall American stopped beside me and asked what I was doing! His name, Hank, I explained that I was trying to get to Beira **"there's a war on"** he replied. **"I know but I believe God has sent me there."** I did not know this man from Adam, yet here was I talking to a complete stranger, **"Why?"** He asked. I briefly told him of the work that was to be done at the hospital, the man looked thoughtful, **"I'll take you."** He was going over five hundred miles in the opposite direction, using the very plane that I had originally hired.

They turned out to be 'World Vision' and not only took me to Beira airport and paid the landing fees, but saw me through the formalities until I was standing in the large entrance hall of the airport. Reality dawned on me, between the airport and the city was seven or eight miles of hostile territory! What could I do? Suddenly a red cross ambulance turned up, looking for a patient, there was no one but myself at that terminal, so I climbed aboard and the ambulance took me to the doors of the hospital in safety! I slept in an old caravan for the night, the hot air leaving me breathless.

Not so breathless as the morning news left me, the ship had arrived overnight from the UK and our equipment would be available from 2.30pm in the afternoon! God's amazing timing. I could not have known **"the day nor the hour"** of the arrival of that equipment. We unpacked everything and only one small item was broken and that relatively unimportant.

For the rest of the week I worked with a good team and we prepared for the installation of a medium sized water purification plant, into a new brick built building. The foundations were dug during that week and I left for Zimbabwe knowing that every item of material and equipment was available to the keen workers. With difficulty I managed the trip a few weeks later using a local church leader John and his own car. On the way to Beira we took a detour. **"Some friends of mine have opened up an Orphanage just off the main road."** He said, **"Lets go and see them".**

We turned off the road into a grove of high eucalyptus trees, even through the window of the car the beautiful smell infiltrated the vehicle and gave me a sort of peace and tranquillity. It was very difficult to keep alert in these beautiful surroundings as a false security comes into your mind, allowing you to illogically think that nothing could take place at that time and all is well!

Chinoi Mozambique

We came to the orange groves surrounding the farm and continued to drive across the orchard on the rough track leading from the main road.

Rivers of Living Water by Alan J. Clarredge

The orange orchard

At the farm some two miles into the lane we met a number of army lorries, my heart missed a beat, which army, them or us?

The distinctive Zimbabwe accents gave me hope, as several of the soldiers came in our direction. **"Where have you come from?"** The officer in charge asked. **"Across there."** John pointed out the winding path. **"That's a minefield!!"** The man exclaimed. Then the truth came out as we looked around, during the past few hours there had been a raid on the Orange Tree Orphanage and the evidence was all too obvious. Bayonet holes in the doors, damaged walls, bullet holes through the windows and a number of large holes in the ground, no doubt from some sort of grenade. On questioning the men, it appeared that shortly after dawn, whilst the people in the farm were preparing breakfast, the rebels had attempted to break into the building.

A noise had disturbed them and they managed to put thirty to forty children with a few national helpers through the windows, they rolled along the ground into narrow, brush covered trenches in which they laid and covered themselves up completely.

The shelter for the children

Roy and Trish, the Zimbabwean missionaries at the farm, told the children to be quiet and then re entered the house, it was unlikely that the rebels would kill white people, but the children, who had already witnessed the massacre of their parents and the black workers providing they were not caught, would then be spared. The bandits had duly arrived and decided to take Trish and Roy, two white Zimbabwean girls, one British, and one American girl helping out during their gap years, plus a seventy eight year old woman to be hostages, sadly she was only staying with them for a few days, or so she thought. *(They remained captive until the Swedish legation negotiated their release)* they walked miles during that six months, yet none of them, including the elderly lady, met with any harm!

By the time we arrived the children and the black workers had crawled from their makeshift grass shelters, some were sobbing, others were so traumatised they could not speak. I am told that many of these had not spoken since their parents had been massacred, the bandits used to kill and rape the parents in front of the children, then if the children were old enough they were forced to bury them. After this, many of the children had fingers removed **"so that they would not forget the rightful ruling party of the country"**, as if they could

Rivers of Living Water   by Alan J. Clarredge

forget!! Those strong enough ran into the bush, to be killed by animals or to starve to death.

Many had by some miraculous instinct found their way to this little sanctuary and I silently promised I would bring clothes for these ragged little children. *(Most of the people were only dressed in old sacks)*. After helping the remainder of the workers to get straight, John and myself had to cross the minefield! It was no light matter that the soldiers sat on the front wings of the car, as slowly we retraced our tread marks back down the windy track and onto the road home.

Back to work and one morning I was quite surprised to see a small headline in 'The Herald' "British water engineer, sent by the Zimbabwe Government to supply water to Beira Hospital", the government had jumped on the bandwagon and publicity of the project had commenced.

Lilian was back in Zimbabwe with me, Amanda my daughter was at University in Keele, my son was back at work in the UK. It was to be her first trip to Mozambique, to the farm, we had borrowed a Japanese 'Sunny' from the leader of 'The One Way' Christian Fellowship in Mutare, and at the owners request, could we **"please drive carefully"**. We set out from the beautiful mountainous town of Mutare, set in the Eastern Highlands of Zimbabwe, situated on the Mozambique Border, a short journey from peace and serenity to a war racked territory. The car was full of clothes that we had collected from the UK for the children at the orphanage. The journey proved pretty uneventful until we reached 'Chinoi' and we stopped to look at a ruined church. Within a few moments the car was surrounded by children, they all looked sad, the large black eyes staring up at us in the hope that perhaps we might have something for them. It was all I could do to stop my wife giving out the promised clothes for the orphanage.

Malnutrition was obvious throughout the country and noticeable as we saw the children. The clothes were duly delivered to the right destination and we watched the 'python' salad being given to the orphaned children. Around the walls were the tell tell signs of the attack, bullet holes, ripped curtains and a visual picture of a testimony of God's Grace to those well looked after children. Walking through the high and dense elephant grass (**ten foot high at the very least**) on a long windy track to see the water source for the farm, we wondered what if any dangerous creature was looking through the tightly knitted grass? Animal, or human!!

Orange Farm Orphanage

Starvation was always around the corner and so common sense prevailed, Roy sent the garden boy out into the bush, thankfully he had caught a ten foot python in the thicket and although a python is a protected reptile, when you are starving it tastes good! They used about ten inches a day and it fed all the children for two weeks! *(The taste is not unlike that of a chicken.)*

We had seventy miles to get back to the border along the dreaded Beira corridor with two hours before the border gate would be locked! I panicked, for if we missed the border, then we would have to sleep in the car, far too dangerous. I put my foot down and prayed that we would miss every pothole on the road. Neither of us had ever seen potholes like it before, and with someone else's car I had to be doubly careful!

Flooded Beira Corridor

From evidence we received on our return to Zimbabwe, we discovered that within a few minutes of us passing through Chinoi, one of small towns, on the road, the main thoroughfare had been destroyed by a bomb. We would certainly have been in serious trouble if we had not passed that point in the road. As we reached the border I could see the gate shutting, five minutes early, I begged the girl closing the entrance to let us in, somewhat unwillingly she did and then only on the condition that we would give her a lift home after she finished work. We were only too glad to give the stocky young woman a lift!

Our final journey to Mozambique was a triumphant trip, for at the end of it we were to see a miracle of God's provision for the starving people. This was the season when their rice would be ready. I had seen the paddy fields for some time and there was great excitement among the people as they had planted to reap the first harvest in many years. The road to Beira held another hazard, this time floods:

by Alan J. Clarredge **46**

Punge River Floods

As we drove down the corridor the river 'Punge' had overflowed its banks. People sat beside the bridge huddled in their wet clothes, hands covering ears a picture of despair, the thatched roofs of their huts just above the fast flowing river. The harvest, it seemed, had been destroyed overnight in the torrential rains! My faith wavered, not those long suffering Africans, they prayed and believed. The next day twenty of the largest lorries I had ever seen arrived from South Africa, on board far more grain than I could ever have imagined, far more and better quality than any of the fields could have produced!!

Beira was a city without water, no reservoirs so no water supply.

We stayed with a Christian family in a house belonging to 'Siemens' the large German electronic firm, again there was no water and the once full swimming pool had been 'drunk' dry, the house bath was half full of a murky brown liquid which had been the remnant of the pool water and was now, once boiled, the drinking water of the house. We arrived at Beira Hospital and the first fresh drinking water for many years was duly **'turned on'**. What a blessing instead of a few drips a minute of salty water, a full mains supply was on 'tap'.

Fresh water for all

The smart new building built by the local craftsmen looks so stylish compared to the badly decayed buildings scattered around the hospital grounds. Now this smartly painted construction housed the first purification plant seen in that locality for many years and the sheer joy on the faces of the people was a reward in itself.

The completed water purification block

The work in Zimbabwe continued with comical and sad episodes building a fuller picture of life in southern Africa.

By mutual agreement with my employer, in exchange for importing their Mercedes Benz, I was given the use of the car, which you have already read about, whilst working for them. The vehicle was a yellow Ford Anglia and needless to say **'more holy than righteous'**. Rust holes appeared at every point in the poor car's bodywork, although apart from a strong likening for oil, most of the time the engine ran very well. *(On the odd occasion it must be stated that a cyclist could pass me going up a hill, in fact more than one!)*

Lilian and myself had been invited to the Ghana High Commission's annual independence day celebrations at the Sheraton hotel in Harare by the high commissioner, who's envoy lived in our block of flats and probably needed a lift for his staff. We set out in the 'Yellow peril', duly topped up with oil and petrol and slowly made our way to join the procession of Mercedes Benz cars. The procession was a stop go affair and for me it was a case of 'quick, quick, *slow' (not a quick step dance in our case)* for each time the car in front of me stopped, I stalled! Meaning I had to race between the stops to catch up the vehicle in front.

The trouble being that every time I stopped, a small amount of oil was discharged on the road, any worthwhile detective could have followed my tracks better than a blood hound. The hotel was reached, the two ornately traditionally dressed Ghana ladies that we were carrying breathed a sigh of relief, or at least it sounded like that. Any expression of relief was premature, for as we stopped beside the red carpet leading into the hotel, the car let out a sigh and oil spewed from beneath the engine, depositing itself on the beautiful yellow bricks newly laid for the presidents of the countries to disembark on. The officials of the British High Commission turned their back in disgust as the car was removed and the cleaning procedure was accomplished. We found solace at the table of the Chinese Legation who made us more than welcome.

Sadly it was not long after this that Sally Mugabe passed away and the country no longer needed me. My residency permit abruptly came to an end I returned to England with my allowance that I could bring out of Zimbabwe, $898.20 *(at three to the pound in those days not very much, but bearing in mind the inflation rates of 2008 with the exchange rate is Zimbabwe $60,000,000 to the pound, a fair amount!)*Still with an income from my own company in the UK I could survive and it was a jumping board to an opportunity to serve in the UK as well as overseas in the future.

I was invited to train as a minister in the United Reformed Church and took up non residential training at Salisbury Theological College. It was hard work, my day started at 5am and after early morning studies I carried out a full day's work for my own business, then most evenings it was essays or a meeting to take in the church. Needless to say the hard work was well worth it, and I became the Non Stipendiary Minister of Throop United Reformed Church on the outskirts of Bournemouth. From that loving and missionary minded church fellowship the work in Zimbabwe has continued to grow and each year we attempt to carry out a project to bring water and aid to a part of that needy country.

My work for the church in Zimbabwe has increased as the days have gone by and each year I have returned for a short time to take gifts and clothes, even food to the lovely people with whom I once worked.

Our work is small in comparison to the need of that country but significant in the lives of those whom we reach. The work of Rivers of Living Water has raised tens of thousands of pounds, money given to the people of Zimbabwe in a very tangible form, to our knowledge none wasted and the results of the labour, a monument to God's Glory.

Gifts come from many sources and our secretary Mr W. Harold Willis writes to everyone who gives a donation and sends out newsletters for all who are interested to receive them. In 2004 we had an emergency call from Bulawayo to say that the ward had lost its water supply. The money, *(as always happens prior to a visit)* had come in, enabling me to book a flight to Jo-burgh and on to Bulawayo itself.

Since 1983 Mr Abel Waldman chief technologist has always looked after my transport and accommodation whilst I was in the Bulawayo area, now he looks after me when I return to the country.

This was a momentous trip in itself and I was even asked to carry a BBC recording studio to make a recording of what I found when I returned to the country. Needless to say, I did return and managed to fit new equipment, repair and service machines we installed in the aids wards at Mpilo Hospital in Bulawayo during 2002 sadly giving less than half a glass of water per day to the patients in this one area of a gigantic hospital.

Large water purification Mpilo Hospital Bulawayo

2005

Rivers of Living Water   by Alan J. Clarredge

Abel Waldman chief technologist with his mother

Each visit leads to a greater faith venture within the society, with an ever increasing need to supply even higher quantities of fresh water to the hospitals. In 2005 I was privileged to install and fit a large water unit into Mpilo Hospital in Bulawayo and to fit the small repaired unit into Victoria Falls Hospital. Which was appreciated by the Zimbabwean Minister of Heath Dr Timothy Stamps when he visited the newly installed unit at Mpilo.

Dr Timothy Stamps
(Minister of Health for Zimbabwe until 2007)

At this moment we are working to supply better water, as sickness and disease increases, food and help where crops and money fail, showing a very practical gospel to a needy people. We have removed the old equipment and taken it to the once highly visited holiday city of Victoria Falls, where the modern clinic had no proper supply of pure water to the laboratories for medicines

"*Water, water everywhere, and not a drop to drink*" says the old song how true for the many people of Zimbabwe!

New equipment installed in 2005

New equipment has been sent out each year during February and the large wooden boxes contain water treatment plants, pumps, blankets, toys and tools to enable the work to continue. In 2008 we were able to give two complete kidney units to Mpilo hospital donated to us, also bandages and blankets to the needy people. Now we are distributing food as well.
With the collapse of the Zimbabwean dollar it looks as though the work will need to continue and even with a change of government our services will be required for years to come.

This up-date is in 2010 and we have been involved in the work for over 20years May I finish this short history of the work with the words I gave in the prologue from *Matthew 10 : 42:*

And whosoever shall give to drink unto one of these little ones a cup of cold water only in the name of a disciple, verily I say unto you, he shall in no wise lose his reward.

Alan Clarredge

Thank you for helping us

Donation presentation 2008   Mozambique 1997

My thanks to:

My wife Lilian who puts up with me being out of the country.

My great friend and colleague Abel Waldman who protects, drives and organises my work.

Pastor Philip Chigomi who I have know as friend and Pastor for nearly 30 Years also his family at Hatfield AOG Harare.

Mr Harold Willis for the work he carried out as General Secretary for Rivers of Living water until his retirement and total loyalty and commitment to the work.

Les and Margaret Burbidge as they take on the work as secretaries.

Trina Lewry as our treasurer.

Rossmore Gospel Church for their support.

And To the countless donors along with my friends in Zimbabwe.

Alan Clarredge